W9-AAX-490

NATIVE AMERICA

Cultures and Costumes Series:

CULTURES AND COSTUMES: SYMBOLS OF THEIR PERIOD

NATIVE AMERICA

CHARLOTTE GREIG

MASON CREST PUBLISHERS

www.masoncrest.com

Ark City Public Libra
120 East 5th Avenue
Arkansas City Kansas 67005

Mason Crest Publishers Inc.
370 Reed Road
Broomall, PA 19008
(866) MCP-BOOK (toll free)
www.masoncrest.com

Copyright © 2003 Amber Books Ltd.

All rights reserved. No part of this publication may be reproduced or transmitted in any form or by any means, electronic or mechanical, including photocopying, recording, taping, or any information storage and retrieval system, without permission in writing from the publisher.

First printing 2002

1 2 3 4 5 6 7 8 9 10

Library of Congress Cataloging-in-Publication Data available

ISBN 1-59084-435-1

Printed and bound in Malaysia

Editorial and design by
Amber Books Ltd.
Bradley's Close
74–77 White Lion Street
London N1 9PF

Project Editor: Marie-Claire Muir
Designer: Hawes Design
Picture Research: Lisa Wren

Picture Credits:
All pictures courtesy of Amber Books Ltd, except the following:
Mary Evans Picture Library: 36, 41, 43, 44, 45.

ACKNOWLEDGMENT

For authenticating this book, the Publishers would like to thank
Robert L. Humphrey, Jr., Professor Emeritus of Anthropology,
George Washington University, Washington, D.C.

Contents

The first inhabitants of the Americas are thought to have crossed to the North American continent from Asia about 20,000 years ago. Over the centuries, they spread down through the continent into what is now South America. Together, the two continents encompass arctic and equatorial regions, so the Native Americans developed different ways of life according to where they lived.

North America

South America

Introduction

Nearly every species in the animal kingdom adapts to changes in the environment. To cope with cold weather, the cat adapts by growing a longer coat of fur, the bear hibernates, and birds migrate to a different climatic zone. Only humans use costume and culture—what they have learned through many generations—to adapt to the environment.

The first humans developed their culture by using spears to hunt the bear, knives and scrapers to skin it, and needles and sinew to turn the hide into a warm coat to insulate their hairless bodies. As time went on, the clothes humans wore became an indicator of cultural and individual differences. Some were clearly developed to be more comfortable in the environment, others were designed for decorative, economic, political, and religious reasons.

Ritual costumes can tell us about the deities, ancestors, and civil and military ranking in a society, while other clothing styles can identify local or national identity. Social class, gender, age, economic status, climate, profession, and political persuasion are also reflected in clothing. Anthropologists have even tied changes in the hemline length of women's dresses to periods of cultural stress or relative calm.

In 13 beautifully illustrated volumes, the *Cultures and Costumes: Symbols of their Period* series explores the remarkable variety of costumes found around the world and through different eras. Each book shows how different societies have clothed themselves, revealing a wealth of diverse and sometimes mystifying explanations. Costume can be used as a social indicator by scientists, artists, cinematographers, historians, and designers—and also provide students with a better understanding of their own and other cultures.

ROBERT L. HUMPHREY, JR., Professor Emeritus of Anthropology,
George Washington University, Washington, D.C.

Arctic Peoples: The Inuit and the Aleut

There are several Native American tribes living in the Arctic region of the world, stretching between Siberia and Greenland. The best-known of these is the Inuit, who were originally given the name *Eskimo* by their Native American neighbors to the south.

The name "Eskimo" was meant as an insult. In the Algonquian language, it means "eater of raw meat." Other tribes, such as the Cree, who lived in the **subarctic** areas of Canada, thought that because the Inuit ate raw meat, they were like animals and were uncivilized. However, the Inuit actually had a highly developed culture; their way of life was different from those of other Native Americans because they had adapted to the freezing conditions of the Arctic.

Because the name Eskimo began as a term of abuse, it is often dropped today in favor of the tribe's proper name in their own language: Inuit. Some

Coastal Inuit lived in permanent dwellings made from earth, wood, and stone, while inland they made igloos. Inuit women wear hair decorations and embroider their clothes with brightly colored thread.

scholars believe that the Inuit are from a different ethnic group than other Native Americans. For one thing they are physically shorter and broader in stature than the other tribes. Along with the Aleut, another Arctic people, they are thought to have traveled to the region from Asia in about 3000 B.C.

The Inuit, who live by the sea, hunted whales, seals, and walruses, and used the animals they caught for food, housing, tools, fuel, and clothing. They lived in houses of stone, earth, and logs, making beams from whale ribs and covering their windows with the animals' stretched intestines. Farther inland, the Inuit hunted the **caribou** and lived in igloos during the winter; in summer, they lived in tents made of driftwood poles and caribou hide.

The Inuit's whole way of life revolved around the animals they hunted and caught. They ate their meat, used their hides in building houses, made tools and weapons from their bones, burned their oil for lighting and cooking, and fashioned clothing from their skins.

Inuit Costume

In the harsh conditions of the Arctic, it was essential for the Inuit to develop warm, waterproof clothing. All their clothes were made from animal and bird

A sled and huskies are shown below. Traditionally, the Inuit waterproof their parkas and leggings for hunting by sewing a layer of stretched animal intestines onto the outside of their clothing.

The top part of this Inuit woman's boot is made from cloth, while the lower part is tanned sealskin. Fur and embroidery are used to decorate the boot.

skins, and they showed great skill in designing garments to keep out the cold and wet, sewing the skins together with tough animal **sinew**. In addition to being practical, their clothes were also beautiful, and they spent a great deal of time decorating them with embroidery and designs in different-colored furs. This was partly for pleasure, but it also reflected traditional social customs and deeply held spiritual beliefs. The decoration of costumes was a way of marking the differences between people: men and women, adults and children, and people of different ancestries. Traditional styles of dress also reflected the Inuit belief in the spiritual link between humans and animals. The Inuit thought that wearing the skins of animals helped human beings to draw the power of that animal to them. In this way, a hunter wearing a wolf skin could become as stealthy and brutal as a wolf; and by wearing the wolf skin, not only for hunting and everyday activities, but also for ceremonial dances and rituals, the Inuit believed that the spirit of the wolf could be honored or **appeased**.

The Parka

The basic Inuit costume consisted of a hooded jacket, or parka, pants or leggings, stockings, mittens, and boots. In winter, caribou skin was worn, and in summer, sealskin. Caribou skin was better for the cold weather, being lighter and warmer than sealskin. Other skins were also used: wolf, fox, polar bear, and squirrel, for example.

The parka was tailored to fit the body closely, and was fitted at the wrists to keep the cold air out. The hood could be pulled up or pushed back, and had a

The woman's parka and detachable leggings on the left are decorated with fur, colored leather, and woolen braid. Right, a man's costume features gloves made from bear paws, complete with claws.

band of fur around it. Parkas were worn with the skin, or hide, facing out and the fur facing the body. In this way, the wearer was protected from wind and rain by the waterproof hide, while the fur provided a snug, warm layer inside. Some parkas also had an outer layer of animal intestines sewn together to keep out water. The warmest parkas were made of two layers: the sleeveless inside layer had fur facing in towards the body, while the outside layer had the fur facing out.

The Inuit's boots were called *mukluks*, and were made of caribou fur that could be up to four layers thick. In addition, boots and mittens were often lined with feathers or moss to make them warmer.

The Inuit loved to decorate their costumes with different types of fur, leather tassels, and fringes. Their clothes featured rich embroidery in bright colors, such as red, blue, and yellow. They sewed ivory buttons on their clothes. Many of the women wore hair decorations, earrings, and nose rings made of ivory and shell. They also sometimes wore lip or chin plugs—pieces of ivory, shell, or wood inserted into slits in the flesh around the mouth. Tattoos were also a popular form of decoration.

Ceremonial Masks and Costumes

Like many Native American peoples, the Inuit worshipped animal spirits and believed in ceremonies and rituals as a way of influencing the forces of nature. They carved masks out of ivory and wood, decorating them with fur and feathers. At their ceremonies, the men wore these face masks, while the women wore small masks on their fingers.

The most important figure in the Inuit rituals was the **shaman**, or *angakock*. The shaman was thought to have a special connection with the spirits, so that

The Wolf Dance

One of the most exciting rituals was the wolf dance. Alaskan tribes dressed themselves as wolves, using the animals' actual heads as headdresses. The aim of the dance was to please the spirit of the deceased wolf. The Inuit believed that when they killed an animal, they should honor its spirit in this way, so that the animal would forgive them. They also wanted to ensure that the spirit would allow them to hunt more animals in the future.

This Inuit mother carries her baby in her hood. Often, babies are carried next to the skin, inside clothing, to provide extra warmth.

he (shamans were primarily men, although women were sometimes shamans) could help control events. One of the shaman's powers was the ability to see his own skeleton; thus, the Inuit often wore **amulets** or charms with the image of a skeleton on them for good luck when they went whaling or hunting.

During Inuit rituals, the shaman and his spiritual helpers wore many styles of masks and performed dances depicting their journey to the spirit world. The masks were made entirely to please the animal spirits, to honor the souls of the dead animals, to **exorcize** evil, and to ask for good fortune.

The Aleut

The Aleut lived in and around the rugged, barren islands of the Alaskan peninsula. Like the Inuit, the Aleut based their way of life around hunting and fishing. However, because they also traded with the Native Americans on the Pacific Northwest coast, their culture was influenced by their neighbors. The Aleut were more concerned with rank and wealth than the Inuit, and their village chiefs demonstrated their importance through the use of valued possessions, such as tooth shells and **amber**.

The Aleut believed that the sea mammals they hunted, especially otters, were attracted to fine, highly decorated clothing. The hunters wore elegant, elaborate parkas made of the skins of seabirds, such as the puffin and the cormorant, decorated with **talismans**. Their clothes also featured intricate

Craftwork

The Inuit are renowned for their skill in making practical and decorative clothing for arctic conditions, using traditional crafts, which are still taught today. In the past, bone needles and animal sinew were used to sew skins together.

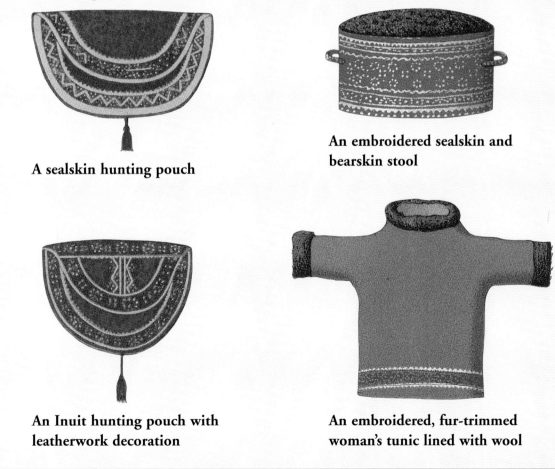

A sealskin hunting pouch

An embroidered sealskin and bearskin stool

An Inuit hunting pouch with leatherwork decoration

An embroidered, fur-trimmed woman's tunic lined with wool

designs using hair bristles and dyed animal skins. On their heads, the hunters wore wooden helmets with long visors, adorned with ivory figures of seals and sea lion whiskers.

Like the Inuit, the Aleut believed that an animal skin could give the human wearer the powers of the original animal. Thus, they made garments so that the parts would correspond to those of the animal. For example the animal's legs would be used for pants or sleeves, while the back would make the back of the coat, and so on. They often left the tail as a flap at the back. Seams were decorated with skins of contrasting colors, because the Aleut believed that the souls of animals lived in the joints of their bodies.

Today

In the 17th and 18th centuries, the Arctic region began to be developed commercially, changing its inhabitants' way of life forever. Hunting and fishing became intensive, as whaling ships and fur traders for the Hudson's Bay Company came into the area. In the 20th century, Alaska became an important site for oil drilling. These changes in work and trade patterns, together with the influx of European diseases and goods, such as alcohol, brought many problems to the **indigenous** Arctic peoples. Their lands were taken over, and their ancestral hunting grounds were overrun with European whalers and fur trappers. Not only their means of survival, but also their spiritual belief system had been shattered. Instead of respecting the animal spirits and killing only those needed to maintain their way of life, the Arctic peoples became involved with the European traders in killing huge numbers of animals for **export**.

As the Europeans took over the territory of the far north, many indigenous peoples lost their lives. Furthermore, a great part of their culture was lost forever. However, some aspects of the Inuit, Aleut, and Athapascan (see box, opposite page) way of life persist. Today, tribe members still hunt and fish in the area, using guns rather than harpoons, and snowmobiles in place of dogs and sleds.

The Athapascans: Dressing for Show

There were other tribes living in the region now known as Alaska. These were peoples who spoke the Athapascan language and who traveled in small groups of families, mostly in the subarctic northern forests. One such tribe was the Kutchin, who spent the summer fishing and the winter hunting. Most of their clothing was made from caribou and designed to keep out the cold. For example, they wore all-in-one leggings and moccasins. The women carried their babies in the Inuit way on their backs, under big shirts, so that the baby lay against its mother's naked back to keep warm. Mothers also used **cradleboards**, strapping their babies to a piece of carved wood to carry them. In addition to being practical, the Kutchin also liked their clothes to be showy; compared to the other Alaskan tribes, they wore more colorful outfits. Their shirts were fringed and brightly decorated, hung with porcupine quills, tooth shells, and little beads made from seeds. They wore headbands with feathers and jewelry made from shells. They also wore makeup, tattooing and painting their faces with minerals, such as black lead and red ocher.

Changing Styles of Dress

Contact with the Europeans brought changes to the Arctic people's traditional style of dress. Instead of being pulled over the head, parkas now had front openings with a zipper or buttons and side pockets. Women wore dresses instead of pants, or parkas with a short, ruffled skirt at the bottom. As the tribes began to trade with the Westerners, they began to sew different imported beads onto their clothing. Today, few indigenous peoples wear full traditional costumes except on special occasions. The most commonly worn traditional Alaskan dress is the parka, because it is practical for staying warm and dry, but now it is usually made with an outer shell of cloth and an inner lining of fur.

The Sioux, the Ute, and the Iowa

In the Great Plains and prairies of America, there were once many Native American tribes. Some of them roamed the vast expanses of wild country, hunting buffalo and living in *tipis*.

Others lived in permanent villages in houses made of earth and wood; they also grew crops and made pottery. Some tribes lived around rivers in woodland valleys. Others lived in the mountains. Although there was often conflict between the tribes, in general, these peoples led a settled way of life that showed respect for the natural world around them. Their way of life had persisted unchanged for centuries until the arrival of European settlers.

In their traditional dress, the tribes of the plains, prairies, and mountains reflected their respect and awe for the birds and animals that were all around them: the eagle, the buffalo, and the horse, for example. The Native Americans believed that by wearing the feathers and skins of these animals, their spirits would help them by passing on their qualities of wisdom, courage, intelligence, stealth, and so on.

Sioux chiefs wear the feathers of birds of prey to show their high status. This chief's cotton cape (left) is fringed with leather and has two foxtails attached to the shoulders. Full, white cotton undershirts (right) were adopted by some of the tribes.

The Sioux

The Sioux, or Dakota, was a large, proud tribe that, for many years, fiercely resisted white settlers and soldiers taking over their lands. The Sioux fought some of the most famous battles of American history, for example, the Battle of Little Bighorn (also known as Custer's Last Stand) and the Massacre at Wounded Knee. Famous Sioux chiefs include Little Crow, Red Cloud, Sitting Bull, and Crazy Horse. These chiefs were renowned for their bravery, wisdom, and loyalty to their people.

Because of their importance in history, as well as the many Western movies and novels about the period, the costumes and customs of the Sioux have come to represent those of all Native Americans. Of course, in reality, not all Native American tribes wore feathered headdresses and rode around on horses; however, stories about the vivid clothes and dignified customs of the Sioux have made a big impact on the popular imagination, fascinating Western children and adults for generations.

The Warbonnet

One of the most flamboyant items of Sioux clothing was the feathered headdress, or warbonnet. This was a band of beaded leather with bird feathers arranged in a pattern above it. Different kinds of feathers were used, and each of these had its own special significance. Eagle feathers were the most valuable type to have, and they were only awarded to warriors who had proved their bravery in battle. To earn an eagle feather, a warrior had to present himself before the chiefs at the council and tell the story of a brave deed in battle. He would often act out the story in front of the chiefs. Witnesses would be called, and it would then be decided whether to award the warrior a new feather. Sometimes, a tuft of horsehair would be attached to the end of a feather as a special mark of distinction.

For the Sioux **brave**, his warbonnet feathers were of the greatest importance. They marked his standing within the tribe and told the story of his

The bear claw and animal hair necklace (left) and the dramatic headdress (right) show bravery and skill in battle. The headdress is made of feathers and red-dyed leather strips that fall to the waist.

The Ghost Shirt

By the end of the 1880s, the power of the Sioux nation had been completely broken. Many tribe members had been killed in the wars. Those who remained had been ordered to live on reservations. In 1888, a Paiute Indian named Wovoka started a new religion based on the ghost dance, a ceremony to honor the spirits of the dead. He claimed that the world would end and a new one would begin, one in which Native Americans, including the dead, would rise up again. His religion offered hope to the poor, demoralized, and fragmented tribes living on the reservations. Kicking Bear and Short Bull were two medicine men who adopted this movement, claiming that wearing a special shirt, the ghost shirt, could stop the white man's bullets. The authorities, who feared a tribal uprising, soon banned the ghost dance religion. Arrests were made, and many were shot. The quelling of the ghost dance movement marked an end to the Plains wars.

life. Some of the great chiefs won so many honors that they wore a double row of feathers in their warbonnet, which trailed down to the ground.

The Sioux also wore beautiful robes made of buffalo skin. For riding, they wore **buckskin** leggings and **tunics** decorated with long fringes and colored beadwork. Porcupine quills and moose-hair embroidery were also used to decorate clothes and bags. Jewelry was often made of human and animal bones, which were thought to bring good luck.

Sioux beadwork is famous for its intricate designs. Originally, the designs were of geometric patterns and made of bone, shell, and seeds. However, in the 15th century, European traders introduced glass beads to the tribes. In the 19th century, Sioux designs changed, reflecting the tastes of other tribes and of Europeans, and floral patterns became popular.

This Ute chief wears a hunting vest with sleeves fringed at the wrists; the front of the vest is decorated with a breastplate of feathers and dyed strips of leather.

Today, the Sioux live on reservations in North and South Dakota, in Minnesota, Nebraska, and Montana. There are no reservations in Wyoming, which was once home to many tribes. Much of the Sioux culture has been lost. However, their costume, especially the warbonnet, remains a powerful symbol of their remarkable history of resistance.

Mountain and Prairie Indians: The Ute

The Ute were among those tribes whose way of life survived for a long time after European-American settlement. They lived in what is known as the Plateau and Basin Region west of the Great Plains. Many of the Ute tribe lived in the arid, mountainous areas of eastern Idaho, western Wyoming, eastern Utah, and eastern Colorado. They had a culture similar to the Plains Indians. They were **nomads** who moved around on horses, pitching *tipis* and hunting big game, such as the buffalo. Others of the Ute tribe lived in the desert. The Ute of south Oregon, western Idaho, Nevada, and western Utah were **hunter-gatherers** whose way of life had survived unchanged for hundreds of years. They collected wild foodstuffs and hunted according to the seasons. The harsh conditions of life in the mountains, and especially the desert, made it difficult for white settlers to dominate their territories, which is why their culture survived for so long.

Like the Plains Indians, such as the Sioux, the Ute traveled light and had few possessions. Women made all the clothing for the tribe, as well as baskets and other containers. Men made weapons, hide paintings, and objects out of stone, wood, and horn. The women developed special methods of tanning hides for clothing, soaking the skins with oils and with the brains of the animal to produce deer or buckskin leather that was quite soft. The women also used bright, effective dyes. The garments they made out of these beautiful skins were simple; often, two skins would be sewn together to make a dress, shirt, or tunic in such a way that two of the animal's legs would form sleeves and the other two would be left hanging down the sides of the garment. The women did not use needles, but pierced holes in the skins with a piece of sharp bone called an awl; the thread—usually made of animal sinew but sometimes of vegetable fiber fashioned into a cord—would then be passed through the holes.

Ute men wore a small cloth around their waist and loins called a breechcloth. In hot weather, they

This Sioux chief's son is wearing cotton moccasins and decorated woolen leggings. Male tribe members other than chiefs wore wild cock, pheasant, and other bird feathers in their hair.

wore little else, but in the winter, they wore leather shirts and leggings. Women wore fringed dresses and, in the winter, leggings. In cold weather, both men and women wore light, warm rabbit-skin blankets made out of thin strips of hide with the fur left on. They also wore moccasins, soft shoes with no heel that were usually highly decorated with beads. In the mountains, the tribes made

Ute Beadwork

The Ute were famous for the bead embroidery on their clothing and accessories, such as pouches and bags. In addition to decorating their garments with fringes cut into the leather, with hair tassels and bunches, with shells, and with elk teeth, they made geometric patterns on them using beads of different colors. The classic Ute style was to use black and white, or a few strong primary colors, against a light background.

The Ute were using glass beads acquired from traders before they had contact with Western settlers in the early 19th century. From that time on, they used "pony beads," so-called because they were brought on pack ponies. These were Italian beads manufactured in Venice. Later, in the 19th century, the Ute began to use "seed beads," small glass beads that enabled them to do finer, more intricate work. Instead of geometric designs, they began to use curved lines, making abstract floral patterns. Later, their floral designs became less abstract and more realistic.

The decorative beads were used on a variety of garments. They adorned the upper part, or yokes, of the women's dresses, or were sewn in strips onto men's shirts. Beaded strips were also added to the sides of leggings. Moccasins were heavily decorated, as were children's clothes. Men wore pouches, in which they kept tobacco and items for lighting fires and for face painting. Women's pouches usually contained combs and materials for sewing the family clothes. These pouches were heavily decorated, too.

Unlike many other tribes, Ute men do not wear feathered headdresses, because they consider the shape of their skulls and their long, dark hair to be a sign of beauty.

moccasins with a tough leather sole. In the late 19th century, the Ute, along with other Native American tribespeople, began to wear cloth shirts, which the white settlers introduced to them.

The Ute carried their babies in a type of portable crib made of a wooden frame covered in soft hide. The baby lay in a little pouch, with its head protected by a hood made of woven willow bark. Behind this was an arched frame, also made of willow bark. The crib had a strap on the back so that it could be carried on a person's back, slung onto the saddle of a horse, or hung up in a tent. The cribs were usually beautifully decorated, dyed bright colors, and embroidered with beads.

The Native Americans of the plains, mountains, and prairies all prided themselves on their hair. They wore their hair long and dressed it in a variety of styles, including beaded braids. Apart from the warbonnets they wore for battle, the men usually went bareheaded, wearing only beaded headbands.

The Iowa

The Iowa lived in the state that now bears their name. The name derives from a word in the Siouan language, *ayuhwa*, meaning "sleepy ones." Legend has it that the tribe once lived in the Great Lakes region, united with other Siouan-speaking tribes, such as the Winnebago, the Oto, and the Missouri. They then migrated to the prairies and lived there in wood-frame houses, hunting the buffalo. When they began using horses, their culture became more like that of the Plains Indians. They were forced to move around a lot because of aggression from other tribes and from white settlers. At the beginning of the 18th century, they lived near the Red Pipestone Quarry in southwestern Minnesota, collecting a material called catlinite to make pipes.

Many Native American tribes used tobacco for ceremonies. The ritual of smoking was thought by the tribes to lift the spirit up to the sky. Different materials were used for pipes, but the most popular was a red type of stone called catlinite, named after George Catlin, who visited the quarry in 1835 and brought a sample back for scientific analysis. Catlinite had been known to Native Americans from prehistoric times, and was used to make all kinds of elaborate pipes. The stem and bowl were usually made in two parts and were carried in a decorated bag; when they were put together for smoking, the pipe was believed to have sacred power.

The "pipe tomahawk," which featured a smoking bowl and a hollowed handle, was developed by white settlers for trade and became a status symbol among Native American chiefs.

The Fox, the Sauk, and the Hupa

The homelands of the Fox tribe—the Red and Yellow Earth People—are in the region of the western Great Lakes. Their name in their own language is "Mesquakie," meaning "red earth people." They named themselves after the color of the soil in their native lands.

The Mesquakie divided their people into groups, or clans, each with the symbol of an animal, such as the deer or the fox. When Europeans encountered the Mesquakie, they called them Fox, probably mistaking the symbol of a particular clan for the name of the whole tribe.

The Sauk tribe had close ties with the Mesquakie throughout their history. In the Algonquian language, the name "Sauk" means "yellow earth people." Like the Mesquakie and another closely linked tribe, the Kickapoo, they lived in the western Great Lakes region.

These members of the Fox, or Mesquakie, tribe wear necklaces made of bear teeth, claws, and skin. The chief (far left) wears a fur hat decorated with a woolen star.

In summer, the Mesquakie and the Sauk lived in the woodlands along river valleys, building bark-covered houses and farming crops, such as squash, beans, and tobacco. In winter, they left their houses to go to the prairies and hunt the buffalo. The Fox and the Sauk, together with other tribes in the area, were known as "the people of the calumet" (a ceremonial pipe), because tobacco-smoking was central to their belief system. They had ceremonies in which they smoked long pipes made of wood and red stone. The pipes were believed to be sacred when in use.

Mesquakie and Sauk arts and crafts were well known for their beautiful designs, which included both geometric patterns and curved forms of flowers and leaves. Like other Native American tribes, the Mesquakie women used patterns on clothing and accessories to instruct the tribe members about the spiritual world. A Mesquakie woman, Adeline Wanatee, who writes on Native American arts, says, "You can see that our patterns are split—we Mesquakie are like that—half in this world and half in the spirit world." She goes on to say that the Mesquakie people are like trees: people can see the part above the ground, but not the roots underground. In the same way, Mesquakie patterns on clothing and baskets reflect the material world of shapes and forms, but also

Purposeful Pipes

"The people of the calumet" decorated their pipes for different occasions. When issues relating to the village and the tribe were discussed, the pipes were decorated with white feathers and the "peace chief" was in charge. In matters of war, the pipes were decorated with red feathers and the "war chief" led the debate. There was also a religious leader, or shaman, who led religious ceremonies for a variety of purposes, from ensuring good crops to curing the sick. In these ceremonies, all people present smoked the pipe.

This Sauk chief is wearing a characteristic cotton turban with feather plume. His cloak has a lining decorated with appliqué, while his trousers are gathered at the knee with garters.

hint at another spiritual world that we cannot see.

In addition to being "split" between the material and spiritual worlds, Mesquakie and Sauk designs show the influence of two different cultures: Native American and European. The Mesquakie were famous for their ribbonwork, in which silk ribbons were sewn onto garments in an **appliqué** design. The brightly colored ribbons were usually cut into curved shapes and sewn in wide bands onto a black background. This style was especially popular for skirts and moccasins. The skirts featured bands of ribbon around the hem, with the cut ribbon in a wide band at the front of the garment. The moccasins had ankle flaps with patterns of cut ribbon running along them, while the front and back were decorated with elaborate beadwork.

Another striking feature of Mesquakie costume was their jewelry. Bear claws were used to make impressive necklaces, usually worn by men. Large, decorative glass beads connected the individual bear claws. In some cases, beads were drilled into the claws. Often, a decorated otter pelt trailed down from the back of the necklace. Sometimes, the pelt was decorated with glass seed beads

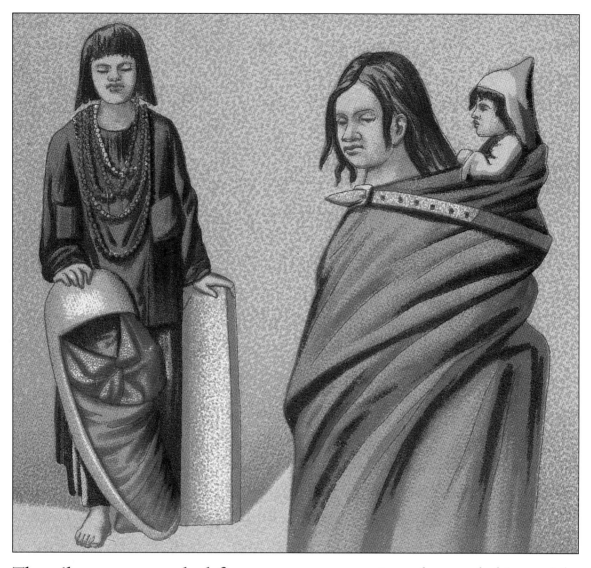

The tribeswoman on the left wears a cotton tunic and a wool skirt, with necklaces of red and white beads. The crib is made of wood. The other tribeswoman carries her child under a woolen cloak held with a belt.

and silk ribbons. These necklaces were signs of bravery because bears were so difficult to kill. Bear-claw necklaces were prized by many tribes in the plains and prairies because of the skill with which they were made.

The Mesquakie and Sauk were also known for their unusual headdresses, which were often made of **wickerwork** and cloth, as well as feathers. Their clothes were made of leather and of cloth acquired through trade with white

This tribesman on the left wears a necklace of carved dentalia shells, used as a form of money, and a traditional wickerwork hat. A woman, right, carries her baby in a basket made of willow and hazel. Her long hair is tied with cotton ribbons.

settlers. They also traded with other tribes, acquiring jewelry, such as silver armbands, belts, and **brooches** made by the Navajo.

The Hupa

The Hupa's tribal homelands were in the Klamath River Valley area of northwest California. Today, they live in Hoopa Valley, the largest Native American reservation in California. Prior to this, they lived in houses made of redwood and cedar, and fished for salmon in the rivers. They caught fish by trapping them in **weirs** across the rivers or by netting them in large triangular nets. They also ate acorns, which they ground into a kind of flour for soup. They were famed for their basketwork and traded baskets, acorns, and other goods with the Yurok, a closely allied tribe that lived in the same region.

Hupa clothing and culture were quite distinct from that of the plains and prairie Indians. The men wore deerskin breechcloths and deerskin moccasins with elk-hide soles, while the women wore knee-length skirts of deerskin with a slit at the front. Over the slit, they wore an apron heavily decorated with fringes and pine-nut shells. The women also wore woven bowl-shaped hats. The patterns on these hats symbolized Hupa culture and were worn on festive or religious occasions. They were made of natural materials of different colors, such as hazel sticks, bear grass, black ferns, willow roots, and maidenhair ferns.

These Hupa women (left and right) wear long necklaces of red beads and fringed aprons decorated with pine-nut shells. The tribesman (center) carries a quiver made from animal skin.

In cold weather, men and women wore over their shoulders blankets made of rabbit or other skins sewn together. Around their necks, they wore long necklaces made of dentalia shells (a fine white shell regarded as valuable by the tribes of the area), which were an important trade item for the Hupa.

Babies were carried in little baskets woven from hazel sticks and willow roots. Inside the basket, the baby was wrapped in a soft blanket. To this day, Hopi people still make these hazel and willow baskets for their children.

Hupa Dance Costumes

The Hupa believed that many years ago, the earth was inhabited by a strange race of beings who took the form of humans. In their everyday life and in their ceremonies, the Hupa quietly repeated brief stories about the origins of the tribe. Hupa shamans were usually women, and, like most shamans, they held an important position in the tribe. Shamans were believed to have magical powers and the ability to inflict or cure sickness, either by dreaming or through ceremonial dances. The two most important dances of the Hupa tribe were the jumping dance and the white deerskin dance.

In the jumping dance, which was an annual ceremony for preventing disease **epidemics**, dancers wore a headdress made of a band of deerskin, onto which many rows of red woodpecker feathers were sewn. These feathers came from the crest of the woodpecker and could number between 20 and 100 crests. They were seen as a sign of an individual's wealth. Around the edge of the headdress was a narrow band of white deer hair. The dancers wore as many bead and shell necklaces as they could make or borrow. In their right hands they carried a cylinder-shaped stick with a slit in it from end to end.

For the white deerskin dance, which was thought to help crops grow, the Hupa wore deerskins acquired through trade with the Wiyot tribe. The white deerskin dance was part of the world renewal ceremony, in which the Hupa and other tribes, such as the Chilula, asked their ancestors for help in assuring food for the future.

Mexican Americans: Spanish and Creole Influences

The large region that is now called Mexico is home to many peoples of differing cultures, reflecting the turbulent history of the region.

Scholars often group the indigenous peoples of Mexico into two main types: those of the Southwest culture, which includes nomadic tribes, such as the Apache and the Navajo, as well as village-dwelling tribes, known as Pueblo Indians; and those of the ancient Mesoamerican civilizations, which include the Aztec, the Maya, the Olmec, and the Toltec. "The Southwest" refers to the Native American tribes who once inhabited an area of the United States

This 19th-century illustration shows the Apache tribe planning their revolt against the United States government. The chiefs wear feathered warbonnets and carry decorated shields and spears; some carry guns.

extending from central and northern Mexico to New Mexico and Colorado. "Mesoamerican" refers to Native American tribes in the south of Mexico, who had a similar pattern of life to some native peoples in South America.

In the 16th century, Spanish explorers came to Mexico to find gold, settle land, and establish colonies. The Spanish campaign to take over the Native Americans' land and dominate the region caused long and brutal conflicts over the centuries. Eventually, the Native American tribes came under Spanish rule. In the 19th century, Mexico gained independence from Spain, only to surrender a large territory to the United States.

After the Spanish settled and ruled Mexico, new social and ethnic groups came into being. White Spanish people born in Mexico came to be known as creole, but this term also referred to people of mixed Spanish and Native American descent.

Over the years, the Native Americans and the Spanish traded with each other. They were often at war, yet their ways of life became closely bound together. In the process, their arts and crafts blended together to create a unique Mexican culture. This mixed culture is especially striking in Mexican dress and jewelry.

These rich 19th-century Mexicans wear felt *sombreros*, short jackets, *calzoneros* (leggings), and cotton or hide pants. The man on the left wears a striped silk *serape* over his shoulder.

This warrior costume of a Mexican Native American chief has metal blades attached to the fringes of his bison-skin tunic, which make a clashing noise when he moves.

Apache and Navajo Dress

The Apache homelands were in New Mexico, northern Mexico, and parts of Arizona, Texas, and Colorado. The Apache were hunter-gatherers who searched for wild plant foods and hunted deer and rabbits. Some lived in dome-shaped houses with pole frames covered in brush, grass, or reed mats. These houses were called *wickiup*. Others lived like the Plains Indians, in tepees. Like the Plains tribes, they wore deerskin clothing decorated with feathers, fringes, and beads. They never grew or wove cotton, but acquired it through trade or through raids on neighboring peoples.

The Apache, and especially their most-famous chief, Geronimo, were known for their warlike nature. They were feared by village-dwelling tribes and white settlers alike. They often made raids on villages and settlements, carrying off food and other goods.

The Apache believed in a supernatural being called Ussen, the Giver of Life. They also believed in mountain spirits, which they called *gans*. In religious ceremonies, the men dressed up as *gans*, wearing body paint and wooden headdresses and carrying wooden swords.

Like the Apache, the Navajo had a nomadic way of life, hunting small game and searching for wild foods. Their homelands were mainly in Arizona and New Mexico, but they traveled throughout Mexico, too. In their own language, the Navajo call themselves "Dine," meaning simply "the people." When the Spanish arrived, they mistook the tribe for Apache, calling them Apache de Navajo (Navajo was the name of the area where they lived). The Navajo lived in shelters called *hogans*, cone-shaped dwellings on a log framework covered in bark or dried mud. The doorways on their houses always faced east.

The Navajo were as warlike as the Apache, often raiding village-dwelling tribes for food and property, kidnapping women, and forcing prisoners into slavery. Yet unlike the Apache, they adopted some village ways. They kept sheep and learned to spin wool, dye thread, and weave on a loom. Their blankets and rugs, which were often worn as cloaks, became famous for their bright colors and geometric designs. In the mid-19th century, they learned silversmithing, and today, their jewelry is known throughout the world for its beauty.

Navajo Jewelry

When the Spanish came to the area looking for gold, they found that the Native Americans had no knowledge of precious metals—they did not even have a word for metal. However, they quickly learned the art of silversmithing. The Navajo in particular perfected the art of making fine silver jewelry using only basic tools.

The Navajo's favorite stone was turquoise. This varied in color from blue to green, and was mined at the Cerillos mines in New Mexico, which are now run by the Santo Domingo Indians. The Navajo traded turquoise with other tribes, such as the Aztecs, and also imported turquoise for themselves from Persia. The turquoise was rolled on sandstone to smooth off any rough edges and then made into necklaces. Silver was heated and pounded into shape on an anvil. Patterns were then made on the silver using stamp dies. Originally, these stamp dies were used to make patterns on leather saddles, bags, and clothing.

This Navajo woman is weaving a blanket on a loom. Navajo artifacts, including blankets, turquoise, and silver jewelry, have been traded for centuries with other Native American tribes and with Europeans.

Pueblo Indian Designs

When the Spanish arrived in the Southwest, they called the tribes in the villages there "Pueblo" Indians, from the Spanish word meaning "town" or "village." These peoples were made up of many tribes, including the Hopi and the Zuni. The Hopi homelands were in what is now Arizona, and the Zuni lived farther to the east in what is now New Mexico. Other Pueblo Indians lived along the Rio Grande, a river that flows through the Southwest to the Gulf of Mexico.

The Pueblo Indians lived in villages on the top of small **mesas**, or **plateaus**, in arid country. Their houses were several stories high and made out of adobe, a kind of sun-dried brick made from clay and straw. They farmed squash,

Shells, Squash Blossoms, and Crescents

The influence of Spanish design on Navajo jewelry was quite evident. The Navajo made "concha belts"—belts of large, patterned silver discs (in Spanish, *concha* means "shell"). They also incorporated Spanish designs when making ornaments, such as squash-blossom necklaces. The squash blossom was a Native American symbol of fertility, but the actual shape of the flower used in Navajo jewelry was a pomegranate blossom. The pomegranate-blossom design had been used in Spain for centuries. It later became a popular shape in Mexico for bead embroidery on clothing, such as jackets and pants. Another Spanish influence was the *naja*, a crescent-shaped ornament used to decorate horse bridles and necklaces.

beans, cotton, and tobacco and kept tame turkeys. They were renowned for their beautiful pottery. Pueblo men wore cotton skirts and leather sandals, while the women wore cotton dresses and sandals or high-topped moccasins. Deerskin and rabbit skin were also used for clothing.

Unlike many Native Americans, in the Hopi tribe, the men did most of the weaving. Hopi men wove cotton blankets that were also worn as clothing. Women colored the threads with red, green, orange, and yellow dyes made from plants. When a Hopi man married, his male relatives were expected to make his wedding outfit. Unmarried girls in the Hopi tribe wore a hairstyle unique to their tribe, with two bunches of hair on either side of the head, symbolizing the squash blossom. When they were married, they were presented with a wedding sash, with long tasseled fringes and intricate designs of stripes and diamond shapes. They treasured these sashes until they died.

Because of their agricultural way of life in such arid country, the Pueblo Indians depended on rain, so most of their ceremonies were rain dances. For these ceremonies, they wore special white dance sashes around their waists,

A Pueblo Indian child cries for the loss of her candy. The child wears a traditional cotton dress with a wide cotton sash woven in bright colors. A plain cotton blanket is worn over the shoulders.

with long cotton tassels on them. These sashes symbolized rain falling from the clouds. They believed in *kachina*, good spirits who protected and guarded them. To please the *kachina*, they made masks of painted wood and leather. They also made little *kachina* dolls to instruct their children about the spiritual world. When children behaved badly, they were shown "scare *kachinas*"— dolls with pop eyes and long teeth.

The Aztec: Costumes of Rank

When the Spanish arrived in Mexico in the 16th century, they found an advanced civilization there, that of the Aztec. The Aztec and their ancestors, the Olmec, as well as the Maya and the Toltec, had inhabited the region for thousands of years and had built great cities there. The main city, Tenochtitlán,

guzmā.   mchv acā.

This detail from an Aztec manuscript shows Mexican Aztec soldiers, dressed in padded cotton armor, fighting the Spanish conquistadores, who are on horseback.

which is now Mexico City, had a population of 300,000, and the Aztec ruled an empire of five million people.

Aztec leaders had strict rules regarding what members of their society wore. Clothes showed a person's status. Their leader, the Chief of Men, wore a tunic of coyote fur and white duck feathers. His clothes were of dyed cotton, and he wore gold, silver, and jade jewelry, as well as a nose ornament of turquoise. He was the only person allowed to wear turquoise jewelry or turquoise-colored clothing.

Aztec noblemen were allowed to wear brightly colored cloaks and necklaces, earrings, and armbands. They also wore nose and lip ornaments. Below them were the merchants, who wore white cotton cloaks decorated with designs. Eagle knights wore feathered costumes and helmets in the shape of eagle heads, while jaguar knights wore jaguar skins, including the head. Common soldiers wore padded cotton armor, or breechcloths and long shirts. They shaved their heads bare, except for one lock of hair at the back. If a soldier took a prisoner in battle, he was allowed to grow his hair and wear decorated tunics.

The Aztec wore sandals made of leather or woven from plants. The lower orders of society, such as workers and farmers, went barefoot and were not

Montezuma II, Aztec emperor of Mexico, is shown dressed in all his finery. His gold bracelets, headdress, and sandals, studded with turquoise stones, show his important status. His throne is also made of gold.

This Creole townswoman wears the Spanish *mantilla* with a silk skirt and satin slippers. To her left, the man wears a poncho and sombrero, with long *calzoneros* (leggings) covering his feet.

allowed to wear colorful clothes. The men wore breechcloths of woven plant leaves, while the women wore plain white shirts and long skirts.

When Hernán Cortés arrived in 1519, he was able to conquer this great civilization in a few years. He began by marching on Tenochtitlán with only 400 soldiers. He won the battle, partly because, unlike the Aztec, he had guns and horses. But he was also able to get the support of other Indian tribes because they hated the Aztec, who taxed their subjects heavily and also killed thousands of people through human sacrifices to their bloodthirsty god, Quetzalcoatl. After the Spanish conquest, Cortés set about destroying the Aztec religion and culture, which is why so little evidence of their civilization remains today.

The Poncho and the *Manta*

Over the centuries, Spanish people adopted ancient Indian styles of dress, combining them with their own styles. One such garment was the poncho. Both Pueblo and Navajo Indians wore the poncho, an ancient form of a simple garment with the dual purpose of cloak by day and blanket by night. The poncho, a square of cloth handwoven in bright colors, hangs down to waist level or below. This garment originally came from the Inca tribe in South America, where it is part of their national dress.

Another native design the Spanish adopted was the *manta*. *Manta* is a Spanish word for a blanket or large shawl. Over the centuries, these were worn as large wraps by both men and women, sometimes covering the head. In the 19th century, Pueblo women wove *mantas* and wore them as dresses or shawls. They used a black background for their designs, embroidering bright patterns around the edges. Today, Pueblo women wear cotton underclothes beneath the *manta*, but on ceremonial occasions, they wear them in a traditional fashion.

From the *manta* came the fashionable Spanish *mantilla*, or "little shawl." A *mantilla* is a fine shawl made of white lace, silk, or cashmere worn as a head covering or veil. In Mexico, the *mantilla* showed the influence of native design and was often vividly embroidered.

The Spanish also adopted other aspects of native dress. Men often wore leather pants and decorated their jackets with tassels and fringes in the Native American way. Today, clothing and jewelry in Mexico have their own unique style, a fascinating blend of the Old World and the New.

Serape and Sombrero

Another form of dress influenced by native designs was the *serape*, a colorful cloak draped over the shoulders and mostly worn by men. Men also wore the sombrero, a broad-brimmed, high-crowned hat made of felt or straw. The name comes from the Spanish word *sombra* ("shade") because the brim of the hat shades the face from the sun. Farmers and workers usually wore sombreros made of straw, while higher up the social scale, men wore white, gray, or light brown sombreros made of felt. Over the years, the brim became wider until it measured as much as 2 feet (60 cm). The style traveled from Mexico to the United States, where it was worn by frontiersmen and ranchers, and was later modified into the cowboy hat.

Other Latin American Tribes

Prior to the 16th century, when Spanish colonists first started arriving, South America was home to about 20 million people. There were great cities and well-organized social groups along the Pacific coast and the Amazon River and in the Andes Mountains.

Away from the coast, rivers, and mountains, there were simpler societies, groups of people who settled in villages and farmed the land, or who moved around the countryside, hunting and gathering wild foods.

When the Spanish **conquistadores** arrived in South America, they were amazed at the wealth and sophistication of the cities they found. Unknown to them, South America had a long history of civilization. From 3000 B.C. on, there had been great civilizations in South America: in Colombia, Ecuador, Peru, Chile, and the Andes. Farmers had developed a complex system of irrigation in the mountainous regions of the country, bringing a constant supply of food to the people, and trading supplies around the country. The empire that reigned when the Spanish arrived in the country was that of the Inca.

The Araucanians of Chile are among the oldest native tribes of the region. The women traditionally wear handwoven striped cloaks; flat, round brooches made of silver; and leather belts with different colored designs.

The Maya

Mayan civilization began in Guatemala in about A.D. 250, and later spread to Mexico's Yucatán Peninsula. The Maya built cities and temples and ruled over large numbers of people. Their society was one in which rank was very important. There were rules regarding what clothes were suitable for each member of society, according to his or her position.

Mayan farmers and workers mainly wore clothes made of *tapa*, a type of cloth made from tree bark. The men wore breechcloths in hot weather, adding a cloak to keep warm in winter. The women wore loose, sleeveless dresses or tunics and skirts. Both sexes in the higher classes of society wore clothes made of cotton. Wealthy people also wore highly decorated leather sandals and belts. Feathers were greatly prized and were often woven into the cloth of cloaks, as well as being worn in beautiful headdresses. The more elaborate the headdress, the more important the wearer was shown to be.

Cotton and **sisal** were grown on farms. The women spun and wove the cotton and developed a way of tie-dying the fibers, making bright patterns on the cloth. They also decorated their clothes with embroidery.

The Inca

Inca civilization began around A.D. 1200 in Cuzco, a valley in the mountains of Peru. Its empire spread until, in the 15th century, the Inca ruled about five million people in Peru, Ecuador, Bolivia, Argentina, and Chile. Like the Maya, they had a rigidly structured society, in which class was very important. Class differences were shown by the quality of clothing and the amount of jewelry worn, and there were strict rules determining who could wear bright colors and rich adornments.

The Inca hunted animals and used their fur for clothes; they also kept herds of llamas to make woolen clothes. The men wore a breechcloth and a short tunic. Women wore ankle-length dresses. For warmth, both sexes wore the poncho, a cotton or woolen blanket woven in bright stripes, with a slit in the

At an Inca wedding ceremony, the men wear tunics and capes, while the women wear ankle-length dresses. Only high-ranking members of society were allowed to wear gold jewelry.

middle for the head. The richer members of society also wore sandals and, in cold weather, woolen caps or turbans.

From earliest times, the Indian tribes mined precious metals from the rich deposits around the region. Gold, mixed with silver or copper, was used to make beautiful pieces of jewelry, which were set with precious stones, such as emerald, agate, opal, and quartz. Jade was also used and was prized even more than gold. Popular pieces of jewelry included the nose ring, or *nariguera*, and the pendant. Gold also adorned their clothing. High-ranking people wore pieces of gold sewn onto their ponchos, and priests wore tunics made of sheets of thin gold sewn onto cloth.

Relics of a Great Civilization

Sadly, when the Spanish colonized Latin America, they destroyed most of the Mayan and Incan jewelry, clothing, and artworks, along with their buildings, temples, and sacred texts. Many beautiful artifacts made of gold were melted down. However, enough jewelry and clothing has been found, mostly buried in graves, to show that these ancient civilizations had reached a high degree of artistic skill.

Much of this clothing has been found in coastal Peru, where the dry climate has helped to preserve fabric buried underground. In ancient times, when a person died, he or she was buried with up to 20 pieces of clothing. Ponchos, shirts, turbans, cloaks, and belts would be wrapped around the body. **Archaeologists** have found cloaks showing designs of animals, such as cats and snakes. The cats are thought to represent the jaguar, which was a sacred animal to these early Indian tribes.

Other Tribes

In addition to the Inca, there were many other native tribes living all over South America. Among these were the Araucanians, a group of tribes living in the fertile valleys of south central Chile. The Picunche lived in the north; the Huilliche lived in the south; and in the middle were the Mapuche. Of these three tribes, only the Mapuche resisted the Spanish invasion in a series of wars that lasted for the next 350 years.

When the Spanish arrived, the Mapuche were farmers growing corn, beans, and squash. They also hunted and fished and raised guinea pigs for food. They kept herds of llamas, which they used as pack animals and for wool to make clothing. Their finely woven llama fabrics were highly prized, and they traded them with the Inca. Today, Araucanian textiles are regarded as some of the best examples of native art in South America. The Mapuche also used metals and precious stones for jewelry, often decorating their cloaks and ponchos.

Just as there are many different kinds of terrain and climate in the huge continent of South America, so there were many ways of life among its indigenous tribes. In addition to hunter-gatherers and farming communities, like the Araucanians in Chile, there were tribes who lived in the rainforests around the Amazon. Among these were the Botocudo, who lived in what is now the Brazilian state of Minas Gerais. They lived mainly by hunting, grouping into bands of 50 to 100, led by men who were thought to have special supernatural powers. The Botocudo believed that there were spirits in the sky who could intervene in human affairs. Their shaman, or spiritual leader, was able to communicate with these spirits. There were frequent conflicts between the bands, which were fought out in duels between men with long sticks. Although the Botocudo tried to resist European invasion, most of the tribe was killed. Today, few descendents of the Botocudo survive.

The Botocudo wore little clothing, but a remarkable feature of their appearance was their lip and ear decoration. These were round discs, known as *labrets*, inserted into their ears and lower lips, stretching the skin. They also wore beaded necklaces and elaborate headdresses made of brilliantly colored tropical bird feathers.

European and Native Styles

Tales of El Dorado, a fabled city of

This flamboyant chief's crown is made of red and green parrot feathers, sewn to a woolen hood. Botocudo wore little other clothing, except for leaf girdles and cotton aprons.

Facial Ornaments

The Guarani, the Caraibe, and the Botocudo are tribes that live in the plain between the Peruvian Andes and the Atlantic Ocean. The Botocudo are primitive hunters who build few shelters and usually go about naked. Children have their lower lip pierced at the age of seven or eight. The disc-shaped *botoque* is the lip ornament from which the tribe derives its name. Ornaments are also worn through stretched holes in the ears.

gold, first drew Spanish and Portuguese explorers to South America. When explorers arrived in Colombia in the mid-16th century, they did, indeed, find common people wearing gold pins on their ponchos and using gold tweezers and scissors for their work. The indigenous people valued gold for its beauty, but it was also thought to have sacred properties. It did not have the same value to them as it did to the Europeans.

Over the next century, the Europeans set about obliterating the indigenous peoples of South America and their way of life. However, despite their differences in status, there was, in fact, a great deal of mixing between native and colonial peoples. Native peoples, Europeans, and also black slaves from Africa bore *mestizo* children, whose racial heritage was a complex blend of all these cultures. In this way, many aspects of native culture survived.

By the mid-18th century, the population of South America had become quite mixed. Plantations and ranches were set up across the land. In Argentina, the men who worked on the ranches, herding cattle and horses, were known as gauchos. They had a romantic and adventurous image, rather like the American cowboy. The gauchos were mostly of native and European ancestry, but they could also be pure European or black, or a mixture of both. Their costume is still worn today by modern Argentine cowhands. It consists of a woolen poncho and long pants with pleats called *bombachas*, worn over high leather boots. For herding cattle, gauchos carried lassos and bolas (leather cords with stones attached to them) to wrap around the legs of cattle or horses.

Just as the gaucho costume has survived the centuries, so, too, can many other echoes of the past be seen in South American dress today. There are still indigenous tribes, particularly in the high mountain areas of the continent, that continue to make traditional clothing for export, using methods that have not changed for centuries.

The Panama Hat

Latin America is known for its hats as well as its ponchos. The Panama hat is the most famous, perhaps, but there are many other kinds, made from different materials and in a variety of different styles. Most of these styles come from the traditional dress of the native peoples and the Spanish settlers or from a mixture of both.

The making of straw hats is a craft that has been practiced across Latin America for centuries. In hot areas, broad-brimmed hats were used to shield wearers from the sun. The Spanish settlers introduced new styles of straw hats, and also made laws about who could make and wear hats, according to their social status. Straw hats were often woven with intricate designs in different colors. In the early 20th century, the Panama hat—named because it was made in Sauza, Panama, by highly skilled women hat makers—became fashionable in

The Poncho

The best-known item of Latin American clothing is, of course, the poncho. This basic garment, which dates back to ancient times, is a square of cotton, llama, or woolen cloth with a slit in the center as a neck hole. However, there are many different styles and variations of the garment, according to different indigenous and Spanish traditions. In Colombia, wool was not known until the Spanish introduced it. Since then, it has become a favorite material for ponchos, and today, silk has also been introduced. Colombian tribes weave belts called *ruanas* in lively, bright colors; however, such tribes as the Paez and Guambiano Indians use gray and dark-blue wools for their ponchos and shawls, detailing them with designs in magenta and black. Other tribes, such as the Arhuacos and the Koguis, weave completely plain ponchos, using undyed cotton and wool. Today, ponchos in a huge variety of styles and colors are exported around the world, and textiles have become one of South America's most important industries.

The traditional dress of Chile is the poncho, worn by both men and women. The finest ponchos are made by Araucanians from wool and chamois and are dyed turquoise, yellow, green, and red.

the United States. Originally, men harvesting coffee beans wore the Panama hat as a protection against the heat of the sun.

The introduction of felt and woolen hats changed the way of life for many rural tribes that had relied on making straw hats for trade. Wool and felt hats quickly became popular among the farming population, especially in high, cold areas. In addition to straw, felt, and wool, Latin American hats are also made out of adobe or tapia pisada, a style that came over from Spain many years ago, and are still being manufactured in the high plains of Colombia.

Other kinds of hat include the lightweight *corrosca*, a broad-brimmed hat worn by cowhands, and the *vueltiano*, a hat with geometric designs in black and

The man second from left comes from Santiago and wears a city-style hat, while the other hats aand costumes pictured are ones traditionally worn by rural people.

white, thought to date back to the Mayan era. Peasants wore these hats starting in childhood. In years gone by, Latin Americans could tell a person's class and job by looking at his or her hat. Today, these distinctions are mostly gone, and hats are worn according to the taste of consumers around the world.

Latin America exports millions of bags and shoes, as well as hats. The *mochila* is a woven shoulder bag that was part of the traditional dress of the Indian tribes for centuries. They are worn either over the shoulder or tied onto a sash at the waist. The bags feature brightly colored stripes or black and white geometric and animal designs.

Another popular item for export is the *alpargata*, a sandal first introduced by the Spanish. These shoes consist of soles in braided hemp (a kind of plant fiber) with the upper part made of woven cotton and with a strap at the back.

Designs vary, from striped uppers on a black or white base, to plain beige fabrics, often with a raised pattern in the same color. Decorative sandals are also made, featuring, for example, woolen tassels and pom-poms in bright colors. In ancient times, the size of these tassels showed the importance of the wearer.

Carnival Costumes

Today, some of the most exotic and elaborate costumes in the world can be seen at the annual Carnival festivals of Latin America. The origins of Carnival are unclear, but many scholars think it started as a pagan festival in ancient Rome or Greece. The custom continued over the centuries in Italy, where Christians would hold an uninhibited costume festival just before Lent, the 40-day period before Easter when people gave up eating meat. The word "carnevale" means "to put away the meat." Thus, Carnival was a sort of fling before the sober days ahead. Over the years, the idea of Carnival spread to other European countries and then to the **New World** of the Americas.

In addition to European traditions, Carnival demonstrates traces of Latin American Indian traditions. The plumed headdresses of the dancers, as well as the sparkling gold and silver threads in their clothes, reflect the costumes of the great civilizations of the Maya and Inca, as well as the exotic tropical dress of the Amazon tribes.

African costume also became a central element of Carnival. In many traditional African societies, dancers wore face and body paint, masks, and costumes and paraded through villages. These customs came to Latin America with the slaves who were imported there, especially to Brazil, over the centuries. Today, Brazil hosts the biggest Carnival in the world in Rio de Janeiro.

In the early days of Carnival, slaves would dress up by putting on old dresses and powdering their faces with flour, while the ruling classes would wear elaborate costumes and masks. Dressing up in costumes of a different class, race, or sex is one of the main features of Carnival, in which people can revel in breaking the social rules of dress.

Glossary

Note: Specialized words relating to clothing are explained within the text, but those that appear more than once are listed below for easy reference.

Amber a hard, yellowish to brownish, translucent fossil resin used chiefly in making ornamental objects

Amulet a piece of jewelry worn as a good-luck charm to ward off evil spirits

Appease to bring to a state of peace or quiet

Appliqué a decoration, often on a garment, made by sewing one piece of fabric onto another to create a striking pattern or design

Archaeologist a person who studies the material remains (such as fossil relics, artifacts, and monuments) of past human life and activities

Brave a Native American warrior

Brooch an ornament that is held by a pin or clasp and worn at or near the neck

Buckskin the skin of a male deer, used by some Native American tribes to make soft leather garments

Caribou a large deer; also known as reindeer

Conquistador a Spanish adventurer or conquerer who invaded the New World in the 16th century

Cradleboard a carved piece of wood with straps for carrying a baby

Epidemic affecting a large number of individuals within a population at the same time

Exorcize to cast out evil spirits by ritual and prayer

Export to transfer goods from one country to another for purposes of trade

Hunter-gatherer a person who moves about the land hunting for small wild animals and eating wild nuts, berries, and other foods

Indigenous a person, plant, or object native to a country

Mesa an isolated, relatively flat-topped natural elevation

New World the Americas (North and South), as opposed to the "Old World" of Europe

Nomad member of a tribe that moves from place to place to find food

Plateau a usually extensive land area having a relatively level surface raised sharply above adjacent land on at least one side

Shaman a holy man or woman thought to have special powers of good and evil, and to be able to cure sickness and prevent disease

Sinew animal tendons used as cord or thread

Sisal a widely cultivated Mexican plant whose leaves are used to produce a strong durable white fiber

Subarctic of or relating to the region immediately south of the Arctic Circle

Talisman small carved stone or other object worn to bring good luck

Tipi cone-shaped tent of animal skin used by some nomadic Native American tribes

Tunic a simple slip-on garment made with or without sleeves and usually knee-length or longer, belted at the waist

Weir a fence or enclosure set in a waterway for taking fish

Wickerwork work consisting of interlaced osiers (types of willows), twigs, or rods

Timeline

3000 B.C.	Inuit travel to Arctic from Asia; South American civilizations develop in Colombia, Ecuador, Peru, Chile, and the Andes.
A.D. 250	Mayan civilization begins in Guatemala.
1200	Inca civilization begins in the area of South America from the Equator to the Pacific coast of Chile.
1492	Christopher Columbus arrives in the New World.
1519	Hernán Cortés arrives in Mexico; within a short time, he conquers the Aztecs, ordering the destruction of much of their civilization.
1534	The Inca, by now the largest Native American society in South America, are conquered by the Spanish conquistadores.
1888	The ghost dance religion is started by medicine man Wovoka, a Paiute Indian; it becomes a rallying call for Native Americans, but is quelled.

Online Sources: North America

Crossroads of Continents
http://www.mnh.si.edu/arctic/features/croads/
An online exhibition at the Arctic Studies Centre of the Smithsonian Institution's National Museum of Natural History. It explores the wide diversity of North Pacific cultures as well as their historical development from the end of the last Ice Age to the modern day.

A History of Two Moon Meridas
http://members.xoom.com/tom308/
American Indian photos from the Pine Ridge reservation in South Dakota.

American Indians and the Natural Wold
www.clpgh.org/cmnh/exhibits/north-south-east-west
An online exhibition at the Carnegie Museum of Natural History's Web site examining the belief systems, philosophies, and practical knowledge that guide Native Americans' interactions with the natural world.

Online Sources: South America

Abya Yala Net
http://abyayala.nativeweb.org
This site presents information on indigenous peoples in Mexico, Central, and South America, region by region.

Guatemalan Indigenous Costume in Photos
www.rutahsa.com/traje.html
The photos on this Web site give you an introduction to a few of the astonishing and beautiful modes of native dress (*traje*) in Guatemala, and the fascinating and dignified Highland Mayan people who wear them.

Further Reading

Black, Lydia T. *Glory Remembered: Wooden Headgear of Alaskan Sea Hunters.* Juneau: 1982.

Brose, David S., J. Brown, and David Penny. *Ancient Art of the American Woodland Indians.* New York: 1985.

Collins, Henry. *The Far North: 2,000 Years of American Eskimo and Indian Art.* Washington, D.C.: National Gallery of Art, 1973.

Duncan, Kate. *Northern Athapaskan Art: A Beadwork Tradition.* Seattle: University of Washington Press, 1988.

Fitzhugh, William and Aron Crowell. *A Crossroads of Continents: Cultures of Siberia and Alaska.* Washington, D.C.: Smithsonian Institution Press, 1988.

Issenman, Betty and Catherine Rankin. *Ivalu: Traditions of Inuit Clothing.* Montreal: McCord Museum of Canadian History, 1988.

Mails, Thomas E. *The Mystic Warriors of the Plains: the Culture, Arts, Crafts and Religions of the Plains Indians.* New York: Marlowe, 2002.

Valakakis, Gail. *Being Native in North America.* Boulder, CO: Westview Press, 2002.

Villegas, Lilian and Benjamin Villegas. *Artefactos: Colombian Crafts from the Andes to the Amazon.* New York: Rizzoli, 1992.

Wilder, Edna. *Secrets of Eskimo Skin-Sewing.* Fairbanks: University of Alaska, 1998.

About the Author

Charlotte Greig is a writer, broadcaster, and journalist. She has written on culture, literature, music, and history. She is the author of several books, and has written, researched, and presented programs for BBC Radio 4, and has contributed newspaper articles to *The Guardian* and *The Independent*. She has an MA in intellectual history from Sussex University.

Index

Ark City Public Library
120 East 5th Avenue
Arkansas City Kansas 67005